# Counting Animals
# I Spot One

T0025096

## By Julia Jaske

2 I spot one dog.

I spot one cow.

4 I spot one turtle.

I spot one lion.

I spot one elephant.

I spot one horse.

I spot one rabbit.

I spot one cat.

I spot one frog.

I spot one panda.

I spot one fox.

I spot one lamb.

# Word List

| | | |
|---|---|---|
| dog | elephant | frog |
| cow | horse | panda |
| turtle | rabbit | fox |
| lion | cat | lamb |

14

# 48 Words

I spot one dog.
I spot one cow.
I spot one turtle.
I spot one lion.
I spot one elephant.
I spot one horse.
I spot one rabbit.
I spot one cat.
I spot one frog.
I spot one panda.
I spot one fox.
I spot one lamb.

# CHERRY BLOSSOM PRESS

Published in the United States of America by Cherry Lake Publishing
Ann Arbor, Michigan
www.cherrylakepublishing.com

Photo Credits: ©Jose Angel Astor Rocha/Shutterstock.com, front cover; ©worldswildlifewonders/Shutterstock.com, 1; ©Ammit Jack/Shutterstock.com, 2; ©smereka/Shutterstock.com, 3; ©Laverne Nash/Shutterstock.com, 4; ©Maggy Meyer/Shutterstock.com, 5; ©Donovan van Staden/Shutterstock.com, 6; ©Helga Madajova/Shutterstock.com, 7; ©Coatesy/Shutterstock.com, 8; © MelashaCat/Shutterstock.com, 9; ©Ondrej Prosicky/Shutterstock.com, 10; ©SJ Travel Photo and Video/Shutterstock.com, 11; ©Milan Zygmunt/Shutterstock.com, 12; ©Tara Swan/Shutterstock.com, 13; ©ANURAK PONGPATIMET/Shutterstock.com, 15

**Cherry Blossom Press** is an imprint of Cherry Lake Publishing Group.

Library of Congress Cataloging-in-Publication Data
Names: Jaske, Julia, author.
Title: I spot one / Julia Jaske.
Description: Ann Arbor, Michigan : Cherry Lake Publishing, 2020. | Series: Counting animals | Audience: Ages 4-6. | Summary: "Look! How many animals do you see? The Counting Animals series uses exciting and familiar animals to support early readers quest to count. The simple text makes it easy for children to engage in reading, and uses the Whole Language approach to literacy, a combination of sight words and repetition that builds recognition and confidence. Bold, colorful photographs correlate directly to the text to help guide readers through the book"— Provided by publisher.
Identifiers: LCCN 2020003016 (print) | LCCN 2020003017 (ebook) | ISBN 9781534168343 (paperback) | ISBN 9781534171862 (pdf) | ISBN 9781534173705 (ebook)
Subjects: LCSH: Counting—Juvenile literature. | Animals—Miscellanea—Juvenile literature.
Classification: LCC QA113 .J394 2020  (print) | LCC QA113  (ebook) | DDC 513.2/11—dc23
LC record available at https://lccn.loc.gov/2020003016
LC ebook record available at https://lccn.loc.gov/2020003017

Cherry Lake Publishing Group would like to acknowledge the work of the Partnership for 21st Century Learning, a Network of Battelle for Kids. Please visit http://www.battelleforkids.org/networks/p21 for more information.

Printed in the United States of America
Corporate Graphics